United States Presidents

Harry S. Truman

Series Consultant:
Don M. Coerver, professor of history
Texas Christian University, Fort Worth, Texas

Michael A. Schuman

Enslow Publishers, Inc.

44 Fadem Road	PO Box 38
Box 699	Aldershot
Springfield, NJ 07081	Hants GU12 6BP
USA	UK

Acknowledgments

Many thanks to the staff at the Keene Public Library; the library staff at Keene State College; Michael Mann at Harry S. Truman National Historic Site; Liz Safly, Pauline Testerman, and Randy Sowell at the Harry S. Truman Library; and Hal Walsh at the Truman Little White House in Key West.

1

THE SURPRISE
OF THE CENTURY

N obody thought that Harry Truman could win. Nobody, that is, except Harry Truman.

The year was 1948, and President Truman—a Democrat—was running for another term as President of the United States. His Republican opponent was Thomas E. Dewey, governor of New York. Poll after poll reported that Dewey would easily defeat Truman.

Three weeks before the election, *Newsweek* magazine took a survey of fifty political writers. The magazine staff asked the writers who they thought would win. All fifty writers picked Dewey. It was Dewey, 50; Truman, 0.

Truman was on the campaign trail in Indiana when that survey was published. Upon seeing it, he said to an aide, "I know every one of these 50 fellows. There isn't one of them has sense enough to pound sand in a rat hole."[1]

Truman had not become President in the usual way. He was Vice President under Franklin D. Roosevelt. He served less than three months when Roosevelt died in April 1945.

As a result of Roosevelt's death, Truman became President. Although he had served nearly four full years by the election of 1948, Truman was seen by many Americans as an accidental President. They felt that he had not earned his way into the office by being directly elected by the people.

He was also unfavorably compared to Roosevelt. For twelve years Roosevelt was President. Roosevelt was viewed as larger than life by many Americans. He was a well-educated man from a wealthy background. He graduated from Harvard University and was a successful businessperson in New York City before entering politics. As President, Roosevelt led the country through two great crises. One was the Great Depression of the 1930s, the worst economic disaster in the country's history. The other was World War II, which lasted from 1939 to 1945.

Unlike Roosevelt's family, Truman's had to scrape for every dollar it earned. Truman never attended college. He failed in his career choices of farmer and store owner before running for political office. To many, Truman was an uneducated farm boy from Missouri who could never fill Franklin Roosevelt's giant shoes.

To make matters worse, in 1948 the Democratic party was sorely divided. Conservative Senator Strom Thurmond of South Carolina felt that Truman was too liberal on civil rights issues. Thurmond left the Democrats to run against Truman with a third party, called the State's Rights party, or the "Dixiecrats."

Another Democrat, Henry Wallace, split from Truman. Wallace was Roosevelt's Vice President before Truman. He thought that Truman was not liberal enough, especially regarding foreign policy. He also bolted from the Democrats to run with yet another party, called the Progressive party.

With Truman's sagging popularity and with his party split three ways, it seemed impossible that he could be reelected. Just before the election, *Life* magazine ran a cover story about Dewey, calling him "the next President."

Yet something interesting was happening as the campaign progressed. Truman spoke forcefully. He made chopping motions with his hands to drive home points. He did not mince words. He urged his listeners with hard-hitting messages such as, "I must have your help. You must get in and push and win this election. The country can't afford another Republican Congress."[2]

His audiences were enthusiastic. During one speech in Seattle, a man in the crowd called out, "Give 'em hell, Harry. We'll take 'em."[3]

The phrase "Give 'em hell, Harry" became an unofficial slogan for the Truman campaign. It seemed appropriate for Truman's tough style of campaigning. People shouted it at campaign stop after campaign stop. One time Truman responded, "I have never deliberately given anybody hell. I just tell the truth on the opposition and they think it's hell."[4]

Standing in the St. Louis train station, Harry S. Truman (with Bernard F. Dickman) holds up the Chicago Tribune *on the morning after winning the 1948 presidential election. The faulty headline read, "DEWEY DEFEATS TRUMAN."*

Truman also addressed the needs of each audience. In Iowa he discussed issues important to farmers. In Michigan he talked about problems facing auto workers.

On the other hand, Dewey felt that all he needed to do was protect his lead. He spoke very generally, trying to say nothing that would offend anyone.

In doing so, Dewey was not making strong statements. That tactic hurt him. As election day neared, Truman had picked up points in the polls. However, it seemed too little, too late. Experts continued to say that Dewey would win with ease.

On election night, early returns showed the election to be surprisingly close. Yet as late as midnight, newscasters continued to predict Dewey as the winner.

In the deep darkness of the early morning hours, things began to look brighter for Truman. He had won all but four of the southern states, which went to Thurmond. He was leading in crucial states in the Midwest and in the state of California.

At 8:30 the next morning, victory became official. Ohio went for Truman, giving him enough electoral votes to win. At 11:14 A.M. Dewey conceded. Truman had proven the experts wrong.

2

MULE TRADER'S SON

Harry S. Truman grew up in an America of long ago. He was born on May 8, 1884, in the downstairs bedroom of a frame house in the southwestern Missouri town of Lamar.

It was a cozy house. It had six rooms and was a story and a half high. There was no running water, electricity, or bathroom. Instead of a bathroom there was an outhouse.

At the time most people in western Missouri had experienced firsthand the Wild West of legend. In 1884 Lamar was no longer on the frontier, but the town still had an Old West flavor. Harry's father John Anderson Truman sold horses and mules. His mother Martha Ellen Young Truman, known at Matty, was a homemaker. Legend has it that after Harry's birth, John nailed a horseshoe over the front door of his house, as a good luck symbol. A horseshoe similar to that one hangs on the birthplace today.

The baby boy was named Harry in honor of his Uncle Harrison, his mother's brother. His parents also wanted to name the baby for his grandfathers, Anderson Shipp Truman and Solomon Young. Since they did not want to show favoritism towards either man, they compromised and gave Harry the middle initial *S*. It stood for no actual name.

Because John Truman had trouble earning a living, the family moved four times in Harry's first three years. When Harry was three, the Trumans settled on

Harry S. Truman was born in this Lamar, Missouri, house.

Harry Truman was named after his uncle, Harrison Young. Here Truman is shown as a baby.

the farm of his grandfather Solomon Young (his mother's father). The farm was in Grandview, near Kansas City. The farmhouse was just a bit more spacious than his birthplace. However, it came with six hundred acres of land where a small boy could run, play, and have fun.

Truman later said, "I had just the happiest childhood that could ever be imagined."[1] He enjoyed spending his days on the farm playing on a swing that hung from an elm tree. Riding horses was another favorite pastime. He also liked running in the prairie grass and corn fields with his dog, Tandy, and his cat, Bob.

He especially loved spending time with his grandfather. Harry would ride on a little Shetland pony behind Grandpa Young as he inspected his land. Grandpa Young doted on little Harry. Every summer a country fair took place in the nearby village of Belton. Harry's grandfather served as a judge for horse races at the fair, and he took Harry with him. Grandfather and grandson would sit together in the judges' stand as Harry ate candy and watched the races.

As were many homes at that time, Harry's was one where strong discipline was the rule. One time Harry put his younger brother, Vivian, and a friend in his little red wagon and pushed it into a mud hole. All three boys were a mess. He later wrote as an adult, "What a spanking I received. I can feel it yet!"[2]

On another occasion Harry and Grandpa Young put Vivian in a high chair and sheared off all his hair.

Truman wrote, "Mamma was angry enough to spank us both, but she had such respect for her father that she only frowned at him."[3]

Harry's father John Truman was strict, too, but never resorted to spanking. He did have a quick temper and could humiliate his children by scolding them. One time Harry fell off his pony while following his father near the farm. John said that a boy who could not stay on a pony at a walk should walk himself. Harry cried as he walked a half mile to his house.

Harry's mother, Matty, felt that the punishment was too severe. However, Truman later said he felt that the tough discipline was right. He wrote, "Mamma thought

When Harry was three years old, his family moved to this farmhouse in Grandview, Missouri. The farm belonged to his grandfather, Solomon Young.

I was badly mistreated but I wasn't, in spite of my crying all the way to the house. I learned a lesson."[4]

The last major event at the home in Grandview was the birth of Harry's sister, Mary Jane. He recalled her birth by saying, "We heard her cry upstairs and thought we had a new pet until our father told us we had a new sister."[5]

When Harry turned six he was ready for school. His mother decided that the family should move to a town where the boy could get a better education. The Trumans packed up and moved about twenty miles north to the town of Independence. It was just ten miles east of the big city of Kansas City.

It was also Harry's mother who noticed something unusual about him. During a July 4 fireworks display Harry seemed to react more to the noises than the vivid colors. A doctor diagnosed Harry with "flat eyeballs" and said he was farsighted.[6] The doctor prescribed thick eyeglasses. Harry wore glasses for the rest of his life.

Matty Truman also enrolled Harry in Sunday school. The Trumans were Baptists. However, Matty felt that the Presbyterian minister had been very friendly to the Trumans when they moved to Independence. So Harry attended the Presbyterian Church's Sunday school.

In Harry's Sunday school was a girl with blonde hair and blue eyes. Her name was Elizabeth Wallace, and her family called her Bessie. Harry thought that she was pretty, but he was too shy to talk to her.

Although Truman said his childhood was a happy

one, it is clear that it was not always fun. Because he wore glasses, Harry stayed away from active sports and spent much of his time reading. While other boys carried baseball bats and gloves, Harry walked around with books.

Other boys teased him. To mock him for wearing glasses, they called him "four-eyes."[7] He was also called a "sissy," similar to being called a "wimp" today.[8]

Though he had some friends, Harry kept mostly to himself. If not at home he was often at the library. He later said, "It's a very lonely thing being a child."[9]

It was in school where he shined. His marks in elementary school were mostly in the 90s and even

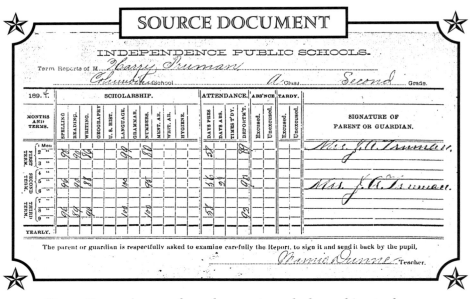

Harry Truman's second grade report card shows him to be an excellent student.

reached 100 in some subjects. His best subjects were language and arithmetic.

In 1896, when Harry was eleven, his family moved to a house in a nicer neighborhood in Independence. In the days before cars were common, it was a status symbol for a family to own a piano. To show that he was moving up in the world, John Truman bought an upright piano and put it in the parlor of his new home. Piano lessons at that time were mainly for girls, but Harry did not care. He took lessons and became a fine piano player.

As Harry matured, he made more friends. One was a boy named Charlie Ross, who was like Harry in several ways. Charlie was shy and loved to read. Harry's best friends, though, were his female cousins Ethel and Nellie Noland.

Throughout elementary school, Harry continued to have a crush on Bessie Wallace. Bessie seemed to be everything Harry was not. She was popular, good looking, a fine dancer, and a superb athlete. Bessie could embarrass her brothers by beating them in tennis or by outrunning them.

She was also from a wealthy family. The Trumans' social standing was modest compared to that of the Wallace family. Bessie's grandfather George Porterfield Gates made a fortune in the flour milling industry. The family's money enabled the Wallaces to live on North Delaware Street, where the richest people in town lived.

There was also a social pecking order. Many of the

residents of Independence in the 1890s associated only with people of the same religious denomination. Some denominations were seen as being beneath others. Highest were Presbyterians, like the Wallaces. Baptists, like the Trumans, were about midway on the list. Lowest were Catholics and Mormons.

Just like today boys and girls in the 1890s met at parties. At the time lawn parties in summer and skating parties in winter were popular. Harry was never invited to any of Bessie's parties. She was a Presbyterian and he was a Baptist, and the two groups just did not mix socially.

Because Harry and Bessie were in the same class in public school, they did interact there. When he had the

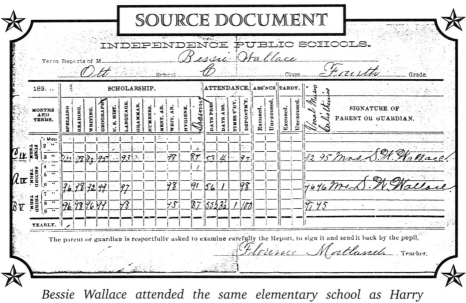

Bessie Wallace attended the same elementary school as Harry Truman. Her fourth grade report card reveals she, too, was an excellent student.

courage, Harry asked Bessie if he could carry her books to or from school. He considered it a triumph when she said "yes."

At age fourteen Harry got his first job in a neighborhood drugstore. There were no child labor laws then to prevent young people from working. Harry arrived at work at 6:30 A.M. and did menial tasks. These included cleaning bottles, wiping counters, washing windows, and sweeping the floor.

The job seemed to separate Harry even more from Bessie's world. Once she was riding around town with some female friends in a carriage. As the carriage passed the drugstore the girls saw Harry sweeping the sidewalk in front of it. A friend remembered Bessie feeling sorry for Harry. Bessie said she wished that Harry did not have to work so hard.[10]

While working at the drugstore, Harry learned about the upkeep of a business. He also learned a lesson about hypocrisy. In the 1890s there was a strong political movement calling for an end to the making and selling of alcohol. This was called "Prohibition." It was viewed as a moral issue, and church leaders spoke in favor of it. At the same time, alcohol was a legal treatment for medical problems. It was especially used as a painkiller.

Harry recalled that some of the same upstanding church members who condemned alcohol were some of the store's best customers for it—and not as medicine. Harry called these people "high hats." Late in his life he remembered, "All those fancy high hats, they'd say

Harry Truman worked at a neighborhood drugstore when he was a teenager. Here he is around age eleven or twelve.

'Harry, give me a drink,' and I'd do it. And that's where I got my idea of what prohibitionists and high hats are."[11]

Not many boys went to high school in Independence in the 1890s. But Harry, a lover of books and learning, did. Harry was a bookworm who could not get enough of history. He also enjoyed reading books by Mark Twain and Sir Walter Scott. Scott just happened to be Bessie Wallace's favorite author.

Harry graduated high school in 1901. His friend

Harry Truman poses with his graduating high school class of 1901. He stands in the back row, fourth from the left.

Charlie Ross won a prize in English. The English teacher Matilda Brown rewarded Charlie with a kiss on the cheek. Harry said to the teacher, "Don't I get one, too?"

She replied, "Not until you've done something to deserve it."[12]

For his class picture, Harry took off his glasses. He stood in the back row. Far away from him was Bessie Wallace, sitting in the second row at the opposite end of the class. They could barely be farther apart.

3

FARMER, BUSINESSMAN, SOLDIER, POLITICIAN

Truman hoped to attend college. A major setback in his father's finances changed those plans. By making unlucky investments, John Truman lost nearly everything he owned.[1] Early in 1902 the family was forced to sell its house in Independence. There was no way now that Harry could afford a college education.

John Truman felt that his chances of finding work were better in a big city, so the Trumans moved ten miles west to Kansas City. Harry's father found a job as a night watchman.

Harry, now eighteen, also had to find work. After a series of odd jobs, he was hired as a clerk in a Kansas

City bank. He spent two years there before taking a better paying job at another bank. He also joined a local unit of the National Guard. Because the unit was new and hungry for recruits, Truman was admitted despite his poor eyesight.

During this time Truman stayed in touch with Bessie, now called Bess. He wrote letters to her, telling her about recent events in his life. He liked discussing classical music concerts and variety shows that he attended. These shows included song, dance, juggling, and slapstick comedy. They were called "vaudeville," which was very popular until radio and movies became commonplace. Truman liked the shows so much that he took a job as an usher in a theater so he could see them for free.

Just after Truman moved to Kansas City, there was a tragedy in Bess's life. One night in 1903 her father shot himself to death. He was one of the most respected men in Independence. He left no suicide note, and people could only guess his reason. It was known that he was an alcoholic. Some guessed that illness had something to do with his suicide.[2] Neither Bess nor Harry ever made any public statement about her father's death.

Harry lived at home with his parents until his father left Kansas City for another farm. This one was in Clinton, about seventy miles from Kansas City. Harry stayed in the city and continued working at the bank. His boss said that he was a hard worker and careful about details.

Truman seemed to be on his way to a steady career in banking. Then, in the fall of 1905, he once more received disturbing news from his parents.

A flood washed out the family's entire corn crop. Again there was a great loss of money. Truman's father was then offered a chance to take over the operations of the family farm in Grandview. It was the same farm where Harry spent three years as a child.

The farm was a productive one, and John Truman jumped at the chance. The rest of the family, including Harry's brother Vivian, also moved back to Grandview. Only Harry stayed in Kansas City.

He did not stay for long. The farm was too much work for John and Vivian to handle. Harry's family members told him that they needed his help. So early in 1906 Harry quit his banking job and headed to the farm. There he assisted his family in raising corn, oats, clover, and wheat.

Today most of farm labor is done by machinery. In Truman's time, sowing seeds, cultivating, and harvesting crops were all done with horses and mules. Even after he had finished working long hours in the fields, Truman had to take care of the animals and maintain the farm equipment. The farm called for many more hours of work than did the bank.

Truman was dedicated. He paid as much attention to details on the farm as he did in the bank. His mother said that he got his "common sense" on the farm and not in the city.[3]

At first his long hours kept Truman from traveling to Independence to see friends and family. Still, he never forgot Bess Wallace. About a year after her father's death, Bess and her mother moved in with Bess's grandparents at their home at 219 North Delaware Street. The house was a proud and handsome one. It had seven bedrooms, windows with stained glass borders, and a large dining room. Meanwhile Bess became a source of strength to her mother, who felt much shame after her husband's suicide.[4]

As Truman became more comfortable with farm work, he had more leisure time. He used it to make visits to Independence. It happened that Harry's aunt, uncle, and cousins lived at 216 North Delaware Street, just across the street from Bess's family.

One day in 1910 Truman was visiting his relatives. He heard his Aunt Ella say that she needed to return a cake plate to Bess's mother. Truman's daughter Margaret later said, "Dad volunteered with something approaching the speed of light, and the young lady who answered his knock at the Wallace door was the very person he wanted to see."[5]

From that point on, Harry and Bess had a steady relationship. If he was not with her, he was writing letters to her. It was in a letter in 1911 that Truman first proposed marriage. He added, "You may not have guessed it but I've been crazy about you ever since we went to Sunday School together. But I never had the nerve to think you'd even look at me."[6]

Bess turned him down. Historians believe that Bess was not ready to leave her family to get married.[7]

In his reply Truman wrote, "I never was fool enough to think that a girl like you could ever care for a fellow like me but I couldn't help telling you how I felt. . . . What makes me feel real good is that you were good enough to answer me seriously and not make fun of me anyway."[8]

Later on, in the same letter, Truman confessed, "I guess I am something of a freak myself. I really never had any desire to make love to a girl just for the fun of it, and you have always been the reason."[9]

They continued to see each other and write. Harry seemed willing to stop at nothing to win Bess's love.

⭐ **SOURCE DOCUMENT** ⭐

Grandview, Mo.

Dear Bessie: July 10, 1911

    I have just about come to the conclusion that I must have offended you in some way. If being in love with you is any offense, I am sorry but it can't be helped you know. Anyway that shouldn't keep you from being real civil anyway.

    Won't you at least let me know you are not "mad," as Shakespeare would say. I was in Kansas City the other day and attempted to call you up but your phone wasn't working or something.

    We have given up all hope of rain out here. I guess we'll have to eat canned goods from now till next year or else live on wheat.

    Would you object to my coming down Saturday evening? I walk like a wooden-legged man but will probably not be so bad Saturday.

                             Sincerely,

                             Harry

Harry Truman wrote this letter to Bess Wallace in 1911, saying "If being in love with you is any offense, I am sorry but it can't be helped you know."

Since he knew that Bess loved playing tennis, he built a tennis court on his family's Grandview farm.

Harry proposed marriage again and again. In 1913 Bess gave a tentative "yes." No date was set. It is thought that Harry wanted a stable income before marrying. Historians believe that Bess felt she had a responsibility to her family. She was taking care of her mother and grandparents. She had become the head of the Wallace household.[10]

In 1914 John Truman died. At the time of his death, he had a second job as a road overseer in Grandview. The job was passed on to Harry. One responsibility was attending Thursday night meetings of the local Democratic party.

That same year World War I (1914-1918) broke out in Europe. There were many reasons behind the war. Simply, they came down to long-standing hatred among peoples of different countries. On one side were Great Britain, France, Russia, and Serbia. On the other side were Germany, Turkey, Bulgaria, and Austria-Hungary. (Austria and Hungary were one country then.)

For Americans, the war was far away. At first the United States was neutral. For Truman and most other Americans, making a living was their main concern.

By early 1917 Americans were feeling more anxious about the war. One reason was that German submarines were attacking American merchant ships at sea. It was also learned that Germany had secretly tried to convince Mexico to declare war on the United States.

On April 2, 1917, President Woodrow Wilson asked Congress to declare war on Germany and its allies. The United States officially entered the conflict on April 6.

Soon afterwards Truman decided to join the Army. He knew his eyesight might keep him from being accepted, so he memorized the eye chart. Before leaving, Harry and Bess made wedding plans. Truman felt that the wedding should wait until he returned. He said it was not fair to Bess to marry first, in case he was killed or maimed in the war.[11]

Because he had served in the National Guard, Truman was able to enter the Army as a first lieutenant. He was sent to a base in Oklahoma. There he was put in charge of the base store, called a canteen. In Truman's unit was a friend named Eddie Jacobson he had met in Kansas City. Truman made Jacobson the canteen sergeant.

Truman and Jacobson ran a clean and profitable canteen. Truman repeatedly received promotions. But men like him were needed to fight overseas. In the spring of 1918 Truman learned that he would be sent to the battlefields of France. Bess gave him her picture and wrote on the back, "Dear Harry, May this photograph bring you safely home again from France—Bess."[12]

At the same time Truman was promoted to captain. In France he was placed in charge of a rowdy artillery unit (the 129th Field Artillery) called Battery D. The men had kicked around other superiors before. They thought that a short (5' 8") man with glasses like

Harry S. Truman poses in his uniform as a first lieutenant, Battery D, 129th Field Artillery.

Truman would also be an easy mark. They were wrong. Truman was willing to dish out discipline that other leaders did not.

One Battery D veteran named Eugene Donnelly later recalled how Truman introduced himself. Truman said, "Now, look, I didn't come here to get along with you guys. You're going to have to get along with me, and if any of you thinks he can't, why, speak right up, and I'll give you a punch in the nose."[13]

Donnelly added, "He was tough, but he was fair; he was a good officer."[14]

Truman and Battery D saw some fighting in France in the late summer of 1918. The most dangerous incident was known as the "Battle of Who Run." German troops had Truman's men under attack. The first sergeant panicked and told the men to run and leave their caissons behind. Truman immediately took control and ordered his men to ignore the sergeant and fight back. They did so and when the fighting was over, they took their artillery and pulled it to a safe haven. Truman impressed his men for his courage and leadership.

The armistice, or truce, ending World War I was signed on November 11, 1918. Truman was sent home a few months later. On June 28, 1919, he and Bess were married in Independence. They took a honeymoon trip to the lakes of Michigan. They then settled in at Bess's home at 219 North Delaware Street.

The next step for Truman was to find a job. He did not want to return to farm life. So he and Bess moved

SOURCE DOCUMENT

The night of the 19th of August 1918 will be one
long remembered by the men who were in Battery
D 129th F.A. in the big argument. The Battery had
left the training camp at Coetquedon on the 18th and
had ridden all the way across France to Kruth
a village in lower Alsace. This battery had been
assigned a position to construct up on the very
top of the Vosges mountains in the Foret de Hevrenberg
just above Mitloch. This position was on the side
of a very steep hill and was an ideal one for a
battery. All movement was after dark and many
things of interest would always happen when
a battery started into a new position. This position
was Emplacements were started and the guns
were moved into them on the night of the 25th
One of the kitchen detail dropped a can of lard
while carrying it up to the kitchen from the road
behind the position. It seemed as if it could
be heard to fall for fifteen minutes down the
mountain side hitting trees and bushes at
intervals and finally arriving at the bottom. The
cooks went down the next morning and gathered
up the remains of the can getting a dab of lard

This is a page from Harry Truman's World War I diary.

to Kansas City. Because they had success running the Army canteen, Truman and Eddie Jacobson opened a men's clothing store (called a haberdashery) downtown. The store was called Truman & Jacobson.

It was in a prime location. Across the street was the classy Muehlebach Hotel. Travelers staying there often shopped at Truman and Jacobson's store.

One customer who stopped by was an Army buddy named Jim Pendergast. Jim's uncle was Tom Pendergast, a powerful Democrat in Kansas City

After Harry and Bess Truman married in 1919, they settled in Bess's home at 219 North Delaware Street, in Independence, Missouri.

politics. Tom Pendergast, in fact, had the Democratic party in Kansas City under his control. He was known as a "party boss" and the party organization did as he said. A local political party under one person or family's control is called a "machine."

The Pendergasts saw Truman as a possible candidate for county judge. (The title of "judge" is misleading. Judges in Jackson County did not rule in courts. They were commissioners, or administrators.) Truman was a war veteran, an honest businessperson, and a Protestant. (The eastern half of Jackson County was largely Protestant.) Truman turned down the

Harry Truman and Eddie Jacobson opened a haberdashery in Kansas City, Missouri. Shown here from left to right: Harry Truman, Francis Berry, Mike Flynn, and Kelsey Cravens.

SOURCE DOCUMENT

SAVE YOUR MONEY!

We Are Quitting Business
OUR CLOSING OUT

SALE!

Lasts only a few days longer.   This splendid stock of new fall Merchandise, consisting of Hats, Gloves, Caps, Men's Shirts, Union Suits, Hosiery and Neckwear, must be sold at once.

Truman & Jacobson announced their going-out-of-business sale with this poster.

Pendergasts. Business was too good for him to quit the store.

Two years later the country went into a deep economic decline called a recession. Like many businesses, Truman & Jacobson failed.

Eddie Jacobson eventually went back into the clothes business and was successful. For Harry Truman, it was time to find another line of work.

4

A COG IN THE MACHINE

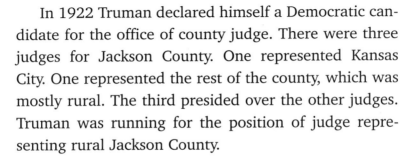

Harry Truman was discouraged. He was nearly forty years old and seemed unable to make a living.

Following the failure of Truman & Jacobson in 1922, the Pendergasts approached him again to run for office. This time Truman said "yes." Robert Ferrell, a Truman biographer, said simply, "Truman went into politics because he was a business failure."[1]

In 1922 Truman declared himself a Democratic candidate for the office of county judge. There were three judges for Jackson County. One represented Kansas City. One represented the rest of the county, which was mostly rural. The third presided over the other judges. Truman was running for the position of judge representing rural Jackson County.

As with any job he tackled, Truman set about to learn the mechanics of his new field. He studied the finer points of speechmaking. Then he learned the tactics of campaigning one-on-one with people. Finally he examined the weaknesses and strengths of his opponents.

Truman gave his first speech on March 8, 1922. The setting was an auditorium in the town of Lee's Summit, just outside Independence. The audience consisted of about three hundred people. Most were war veterans, including several men from Battery D. Truman recalled that he was scared, but added, "It was good for me because I began to learn how to make an appearance before a crowd. It took time, but I learned."[2]

In the 1920s, cars were still new. Many roads were not paved. Several that were paved were done with poor concrete. Some roads were so bad that Truman put bags of cement in the trunk of his car when he was traveling on the campaign trail. The cement helped stabilize his car when he drove over rough patches. With more and more people buying cars, Truman campaigned on a platform of better roads in the county.

He also promised sound and honest government. However, there was more to getting elected in Missouri in 1922 than issues and political skill. The Ku Klux Klan (KKK) was very powerful in rural western Missouri. The KKK is a racist organization formed after the Civil War (1861-1865). Its members became known for vicious attacks on African Americans just after the Civil War.

They dressed in white sheets and hoods to keep from being recognized.

For a while KKK activity subsided, but the group had a rebirth following World War I. Its belief was that the United States was only for true patriotic Americans. According to the KKK, only white Protestants could be considered such patriots.

Because the KKK wanted friends in powerful positions, they tried to make political candidates members. Since there was a large following in rural Jackson County, some politicians joined the KKK to be assured of easy votes.

Like many residents in the farm states and South at that time, Truman thought nothing of using racial and ethnic slurs when he spoke. His letters to Bess even indicate that he had opinions that were truly prejudiced.

In the same letter in which he proposed to Bess in 1911, Truman wrote, "I think one man is just as good as another so long as he's honest and decent and not a nigger or a Chinaman."[3] Truman added, "I am strongly of the opinion that negroes ought to be in Africa, yellow men in Asia, and white men in Europe and America."[4]

In a letter that he wrote in 1918 while in the Army, Truman referred to heavily Jewish New York City as "Kike town." In the same letter, he also called an Italian man a "Dago."[5]

Historians have since debated whether Truman was really prejudiced. It could have been that he was just using words and expressing ideas common for his place and time. Those who believe that he was not prejudiced point to the fact that his business partner Eddie Jacobson was Jewish. If Truman was a bigot why would he be a friend and partner with a Jewish man?

At first Truman turned down the KKK. Some of Truman's supporters told him that was a mistake because he needed the KKK's backing. There are different versions of whether he actually joined. Truman later said that he was never a member.[6]

Some who knew Truman say that he joined to get the KKK's support but was never active. More say that he was about to join until he was told to promise that he would never hire a Catholic. At that, Truman was outraged.

It is said that he responded, "I won't agree to anything like that. I had a Catholic battery in the war and if any of those boys need help, I'm going to give them jobs."[7]

The KKK organizer told Truman to leave the room, which he did. The KKK then became one of Truman's greatest enemies.

With the Pendergast machine backing him, Truman won the 1922 election. As he promised, Truman helped build better roads in the county. He also cut the county's debt in half, fulfilling his promise to have sound government.

At home the Trumans were hoping to raise a family. Bess had suffered two miscarriages. Then on February 17, 1924, she gave birth to a baby girl. That day a winter storm was raging. The doctor, covered with snow, arrived at the Truman home. The girl was named Mary Margaret in honor of Harry's sister (Mary) and Bess's mother (Margaret).

There were political storms in Truman's life at that time, too. The Ku Klux Klan was at its peak of popularity in 1924. At the national Democratic convention that summer, party members would not even approve a resolution condemning the KKK. The KKK was just too

Harry and Bess Truman stand with a young Margaret Truman in the yard of their home.

powerful. Locally the KKK was filled with vengeance towards Truman. It did all it could to see that he was defeated.

Once in the summer of 1924, Truman went to a KKK rally to tell off its members. As he was driving home, he met some of his supporters with baseball bats and guns in two cars. They, too, were going to confront the KKK. Truman told them to go home. He said, "You don't need to use guns. Those guys are scared when they don't have their sheets on."[8]

However, the KKK was powerful enough to see that Truman was defeated for reelection in 1924. The KKK had joined with a group of Democrats opposed to Pendergast, and the group supported another candidate. It was the only election that Truman would ever lose.

Truman dabbled in some business ventures for the next two years. In 1926, however, he went back to politics. With the Pendergast political machine still backing him, Truman ran for the office of presiding county judge. By this time the two opposing groups of Democrats had joined together and the KKK's popularity had weakened. Truman easily won.

Truman showed himself to be incredibly honest. A local newspaper, the *Independence Examiner*, expressed shock that no scandals emerged when Truman was in charge. A reporter for the *Examiner*, Susannah Gentry, later said of Truman, "He walked like he was going some place. And he was, but we didn't know it."[9]

The term of presiding judge was four years. Truman ran for re-election in 1930 and won by an even larger margin than in 1926. He built more quality roads and continued to run the county government honestly. His stubborn honesty aggravated his political boss Tom Pendergast. One time some road contractors and friends of Pendergast expected a contract as a special favor. However, Truman insisted that all contractors be considered fairly. Pendergast told his friends, "I told you he was the hardheadedst, orneriest man in the world; there isn't anything I can do."[10]

Though frustrated at times, Pendergast admired Truman for saying what he meant and being steadfast in his positions. Pendergast himself was like that. He thought that there was an even bigger role for Harry Truman to play in Missouri politics.

In 1934 Truman learned that Pendergast wanted him to run for United States Senate. As before, Truman campaigned by driving. This time he had to drive throughout the entire state. It was exhausting and costly, since Truman had to campaign with his own money.

He also had to compete with candidates from political machines in St. Louis, the state's other big city. Truman won both the primary and general elections. One reason was that people liked him. Another was because the Pendergast machine was the best organized in the state.

In the Senate, Truman almost always voted with the policies of President Franklin D. Roosevelt. The United

States was in the midst of the Great Depression. At its peak, 25.2 percent of the population was out of work. That is equal to over a quarter of the nation's workers.[11]

Millions were homeless. Many who were fortunate enough to have homes did not know where their next meal was coming from. Roosevelt tried repairing the poor economy with a series of government programs to create jobs and provide social services. Roosevelt's policy was called the New Deal, and Truman was a strong supporter.

Unfortunately for Truman, he was thought by many to be merely a puppet of political boss Pendergast. They believed that he would vote only as Pendergast told him to, not based on his views or those of his constituents. Instead of referring to Truman as "the Senator from Missouri," some called him "the Senator from Pendergast."

Truman tried to show that he was under the control of no one. As part of a Senate subcommittee, he helped investigate fraud in the railroad industry. He even found reason to accuse the officers and owners of the Missouri Pacific Railroad in his home state. In 1937 he received a note saying that if he continued his investigations, he would be killed. No one acted on it, and Truman completed his work.

The very same claims of fraud and dishonesty would haunt Truman when he ran for reelection to the Senate in 1940. Tom Pendergast had become a gambling addict and was losing his life savings by betting on horse races.

To get needed money, Pendergast began accepting bribes from businesses looking for political favors. He was caught in 1939 and sentenced to fifteen months in prison. One large state newspaper, the *St. Louis Post-Dispatch*, protested that Pendergast "merited a far heavier sentence."[12]

Since Pendergast had been Truman's friend and mentor, Truman refused to publicly denounce him. He thought that it would show disloyalty. Truman said, "I'm not a rat who deserts a sinking ship."[13] By not denouncing Pendergast, Truman allowed his opponents to connect him to the scandal.

In addition he had a tough opponent for the Democratic nomination for Senate. It was the popular governor of Missouri, Lloyd Stark.

Truman was discouraged, but determined.[14] He said, "I am going to run for reelection, if the only vote I get is my own."[15]

Most of the state's newspapers reported that Truman had no chance. The *St. Louis Post-Dispatch* was typical. It predicted, "Truman is through in Missouri."[16]

Truman still campaigned hard. He especially tried to win the support of African Americans. In the town of Sedalia in central Missouri, he took a very bold and controversial stance by saying, "I believe in the brotherhood of man; not merely the brotherhood of white men, but the brotherhood of all men before the law."[17]

At that time legal segregation was the law in most of the South. Blacks could not sit alongside whites in restaurants and theaters. Blacks had to attend separate and inferior schools. Even in much of the North, blacks were seen as less than equal to whites.

Truman's speech was daring for his day. It was the first time that he would speak out for civil rights. Privately, though, he still used the word "nigger" and laughed at racist jokes, as many people around him did.[18]

Why did Truman continue to use such language? It was difficult for Truman and many others of his time to leave behind the prejudices that they grew up with. What are considered racist slurs today were just slang words to many people of that day. On the other hand, there certainly were people in Truman's time who would have been offended had they heard him use such words.

Truman also gained support from the railroad workers' union. They were pleased that he confronted railroad owners whom they saw as greedy. He picked up helpful endorsements and in a hard-fought battle, won the Democratic primary. He then easily beat the Republican contender in the general election.

Again Truman made a name for himself for investigating corruption. This time his subject was the military. The Truman Committee discovered companies making faulty airplanes and ships. It also learned that businesses were charging overly high prices to the government. The Truman Committee was received positively by both Democrats and Republicans.

With his hard work and honesty, Harry S. Truman had now become one of the best known and highly regarded members of the United States Senate. He also proved that he was no longer under the influence of Tom Pendergast's command. He had won the 1940 election on his own.

5

THE MOON, THE STARS, AND ALL THE PLANETS

T ruman's work against fraud in the military soon took on a special importance. On December 10, 1941, the United States entered World War II. An efficient military was needed for victory.

World War II began when Germany invaded Poland in 1939. As in World War I, Germany was the major aggressor country in Europe. This time its allies were Italy and the Pacific island nation of Japan.

The United States remained out of the fighting until Japan bombed the United States Naval Base in Pearl Harbor, Hawaii, on December 7, 1941. A total of 2,403 Americans died in the surprise attack.[1] The next day President Roosevelt asked Congress for a Declaration of War against Japan. On December 10 war was officially declared.

As the war progressed, Truman continued to fulfill his duties as senator. Italy surrendered in 1943, but Germany and Japan continued the struggle. As the 1944 election year approached, Franklin Roosevelt decided to run for a fourth term as President. However, his Vice President Henry Wallace was seen by many as too liberal. Wallace was especially unpopular with southern congressmen and senators. Roosevelt decided to look for a new Vice President.

Those close to Roosevelt knew that this was a very important decision. Roosevelt's health was worsening, although much of the public was not aware of that. Today any change in a President's health is considered important news and broadcast to the public. In Roosevelt's time, the media generally maintained the attitude that such things were personal. They were kept private.

Democratic leaders close to the President knew that if Roosevelt was elected he might not live out his term. The person chosen to be Vice President might easily become the next President. It was felt that honest Harry Truman would be a good candidate. It seemed that he would satisfy northern, southern, liberal, and conservative Democrats.

When Roosevelt was inaugurated as President for his fourth term on January 20, 1945, Truman became Vice President of the United States.

As Roosevelt continued leading the United States through the war, he left little for Truman to do. That left

Truman unprepared for his role on April 12, 1945, when Roosevelt suddenly died. Harry S. Truman—who was called "sissy" as a child, who never went to college, who plowed land as a farmer, who failed as a businessperson—was now President of the United States.

The United States and its allies were making great advances, and World War II was winding down. Victory seemed at hand. Yet it was up to Truman to lead the country to that victory. Millions of lives were at stake. It was an incredible responsibility. Truman said to reporters, "I don't know whether you fellows ever had a

Harry S. Truman, with his predecessor, President Franklin D. Roosevelt, attends a luncheon on the lawn of the White House. While serving a fourth term, President Roosevelt died suddenly on April, 12, 1945. Vice President Truman was sworn in as President within a few hours of Roosevelt's death.

load of hay fall on you. But when they told me yesterday what had happened, I felt like the moon, the stars, and all the planets had just fallen on me."[2]

The American people expected little of Truman. Few believed that he could take the place of the beloved Roosevelt.[3] Truman did not speak eloquently as Roosevelt did. He did not have a commanding presence like Roosevelt. He seemed to be a very ordinary man. Some said that if Harry Truman could be President, then your next-door neighbor could be President.

Soon after taking office, Truman needed to hire a press secretary. That person would act as a contact between the President and the media. Truman knew exactly whom he wanted for the job.

He called his boyhood friend Charlie Ross, at the time an editor for the *St. Louis Post-Dispatch*. Ross accepted the job even though it meant a big pay cut. They two men met in Washington, D.C., on April 19.

As they reminisced about old times, the name of their English teacher, Matilda Brown, came up. The men talked about graduation night, and the kiss Ross had received from Miss Brown that night. Brown was now in her eighties.

The new President called the retired teacher and asked, "Hello, Miss Brown, this is the President of the United States. Do I get that kiss?"

"Come and get it," she answered.[4]

Fun aside, Truman had extraordinary tasks at hand. Soon after taking office, Truman was told by Secretary of War Henry L. Stimson about a new weapon that was being developed. Stimson said that its power was beyond anything humankind ever before conceived. However, he saved the details for a later meeting. The weapon was the atomic bomb.

There was another important matter for Truman to tend to. Shortly before his death, President Roosevelt was working with leaders of the world on a concept called the United Nations (UN). This would be an organization made up of countries of the world, whose leaders would meet to discuss disputes with other nations. Roosevelt believed that the United Nations was vital to avoid another world war.

This idea had been tried before and failed. After World War I a similar group, called the League of Nations, was formed. At the time America's leaders and much of the nation felt that it was not in their best interests to become involved in other countries' matters. Without the United States, the League of Nations was weak and did not last. Roosevelt had hoped the same thing would not happen this time.

A conference to help organize the UN was scheduled for April 25 in San Francisco. It was suggested that the conference be postponed while Truman familiarized himself with his new office. Truman refused to postpone the meeting, which went on as scheduled. Truman stayed in Washington to work on war matters, but sent representatives in his place.

By that time the German army was on the verge of

collapsing. On May 1 its leader, dictator Adolf Hitler, committed suicide. Germany formally signed an unconditional surrender on May 8, 1945. The day became known as V-E Day (Victory in Europe Day). However, the war was only half over. The fighting in the Pacific with Japan was still raging.

Despite low expectations, Truman seemed to be soundly handling the matters of war. After a month in office his popularity rating was 87 percent, an astounding figure for any President.[5]

In June, Truman took a trip to San Francisco, where he signed the United Nations Charter. This fulfilled Roosevelt's dream. On his way back to Washington, Truman stopped in Kansas City. He took time to visit old friends from Battery D, including his former business partner Eddie Jacobson. The men had fun joking and recalling old times.

Shortly afterwards Truman was on another trip. This time he was going overseas. His destination was Potsdam, Germany, just outside the capital of Berlin. There he met with the leaders of the United States' strongest allies in the war: Winston Churchill of Great Britain and Josef Stalin of the Soviet Union.

Conferences like this were common during the war. President Roosevelt had met with Churchill alone or both Churchill and Stalin. Now it was Truman's turn.

The Potsdam Conference lasted a little over two weeks. The Allies agreed to demand an unconditional surrender from Japan. They also decided to put German leaders on trial as war criminals. In addition they approved an earlier decision to divide the country of Germany and the city of Berlin into four zones. The zones would be occupied by the major Allied countries: the United States, the Soviet Union, Great Britain, and France.

At the Potsdam Conference, Harry Truman met with Winston Churchill (left) and Josef Stalin (right).

About a week into the conference there was a major delay. Great Britain was holding a general election and Winston Churchill was up for reelection as prime minister (the British equivalent of the United States President). Churchill lost the election, and the conference finished with a new British Prime Minister, Clement R. Attlee.

In the middle of the conference, Truman received an important message from home. The United States had performed a test explosion of an atomic bomb in the New Mexico desert. It was successful. Truman wrote in his diary, "We have discovered the most terrible bomb in the history of the world."[6]

Truman's advisers suggested that he use the bomb on Japan to end the war quickly. Instead, on July 2, 1945, Truman gave Japan a chance to surrender. Japan refused.

Truman had two main options to end the war. One was a land invasion of Japan's two major islands. That would mean hand-to-hand fighting between American and Japanese soldiers. The other option was dropping the atomic bomb on Japan.

Truman's military advisers told him that if the United States invaded Japan, there would be five hundred thousand American casualties.[7] If he used the atomic bomb, there would be no American casualties. Truman decided that the atomic bomb was the lesser of two evils.

He wrote in his diary on July 25, "The weapon is to

SOURCE DOCUMENT

HQ U/S FORCES EUROPEAN THEATER

STAFF MESSAGE CONTROL

INCOMING ~~TOP SECRET~~ MESSAGE

~~TOP SECRET~~

U R G E N T

FROM: AGWAR Washington

TO : Tripartite Conference Babelsberg, Germany

NO : WAR 41011   30 July 1945.

To the President from the Secretary of War.

The time schedule on Groves' project is pro-
gressing so rapidly that it is now essential that
statement for release by you be available not later
than Wednesday, 1 August. I have revised draft of
statement, which I previously presented to you, in
light of

(A) Your recent ultimatum,

(B) Dramatic results of test and

(C) Certain minor suggestions made by British
of which Byrnes is aware.

While I am planning to start a copy by special
courier tomorrow in the hope you can be reached,
nevertheless in the event he does not reach you in
time, I will appreciate having your authority to
have White House release revised statement as soon as
necessary.

Sorry circumstances seem to require this emergency action.

(See Over)

ACTION: Gen. Vaughan

VICTORY-IN-733   (31 July 1945)   302217Z   809

~~TOP SECRET~~

B File
1

THE MAKING OF AN EXACT COPY OF THIS MESSAGE IS FORBIDDEN

*On July 2, 1945, Harry Truman gave Japan a chance to surrender,
but they refused. Shown here is a telegram from Secretary of War
Henry L. Stimson to President Truman dated July 30, 1945.*

be used against Japan between now and August 10th. I have told the Sec. of War, Mr. Stimson, to use it so that military objectives and soldiers and sailors are the target and not women and children."[8]

The Potsdam Conference ended on August 2. On August 6 Truman was aboard ship on his way home. It was there that he received word that the atomic bomb had been dropped that morning. The target was the city of Hiroshima, a southern base for Japan's army. The entire city was destroyed. It is estimated that eighty thousand Japanese died instantly. Another fifty thousand to sixty thousand later died as a result of wounds caused by the bombing.[9]

Still, Japan would not surrender. Three days later, on August 9, a second atomic bomb was dropped over the Japanese seaport of Nagasaki. About seventy thousand Japanese died in that attack.[10]

Reaction in the United States and among the Allies was hugely favorable. That was not surprising. Japan's surprise attack on Pearl Harbor was still fresh in Americans' minds. During the war Japan was responsible for brutal treatment of American prisoners of war.

On August 14 Japan surrendered. The formal surrender ceremony took place on September 2. World War II was over.

6

THE PRESIDENT WHO COULD

C elebrations marking the end of the war took place throughout the United States. Yet while Americans were thrilled that the fighting was over, there soon were problems in getting the country back on its normal course. This has often been the case after any long-lasting war.

The term used after World War II was "reconversion." It referred to converting the country from an economy based on making goods to be used by the military to one manufacturing items to be used by consumers.

In 1944 Truman had made a suggestion to President Roosevelt. It was that industry start using extra time and money to make products Americans could use when the war was over. Neither Roosevelt nor the military wanted to do so. They felt that it might dampen the country's strong support of the war effort.[1]

In hindsight Truman's suggestion may have been a good one. Once the war ended there was a severe shortage of consumer goods. The basic economics law of supply and demand took hold. With needed items in short supply, prices skyrocketed. The term used to describe such a sharp climb in prices is inflation. Average citizens, including former soldiers, were unable to afford basics. Houses were especially in short supply.

During the war prices of household items and wages of workers were frozen. That means that business owners, called management, were not allowed to raise either prices or workers' salaries. Most labor unions vowed not to strike. Americans were willing to sacrifice to help win the war.

Now the war was over. Management and labor wanted to be paid back for their sacrifices. Management believed that continued price controls hurt its ability to make a fair profit. Workers felt that they needed higher incomes to be able to buy the few consumer goods available. Through their unions, workers asked for higher wages. Most of these requests were rejected.

Truman's answer was to continue the price and wage freezes. When the supply of consumer items was more in proportion to their demand, he would lift price and wage controls.

Republicans in Congress, led by conservative Senator Robert Taft from Ohio, took the side of management. (Taft was the son of former President William Howard Taft.) They forced Truman to compromise. Price controls were allowed to continue, but in weak form. Laborers, meanwhile, felt they had no other choice than to strike.

Truman was frustrated. If management had to pay workers higher wages, it would then raise prices on products. Inflation would continue.

Though Truman had in the past supported laws that helped labor, he felt that the present situation was different. Truman took the position that a strike would be harmful to the nation's economic recovery.

That did not matter to the unions. Striking was the only way to show that they were serious. For a year it seemed as if there was one strike after another. First there were strikes at General Electric and General Motors. Then the glass makers, meat packers, and coffin makers struck.

Then it was the steel workers' turn. Next it was the coal miners. In the 1940s, the steel and coal industries were among the most vital to the everyday life in America.

Then it was railroad workers. Airplanes were not as commonly used as they are today. People and freight moved by train. With the trains not running, people could not get to work. Food could not be shipped, and it rotted.

In response to the rail strike, Truman made a now famous speech. He ordered rail strikers to go back to work or he would draft them into the military. As he was speaking, Truman received a note stating that the rail workers agreed to end their strike.

Meanwhile the President had his hands full with foreign problems. Despite the fact that the United States and the Soviet Union had different forms of government, both were targets of Germany during World War II. So during the war they were allies and fought on the same side.

Now that the war was over, these two superpowers were at odds with each other. The Soviet Union practiced communism while the United States practices capitalism.

In capitalism, services and manufacturing are provided by privately owned businesses. In pure communism there is no private business. Manufacturing and services are owned by the community. Communism as practiced in the Soviet Union was different. All business and property were owned by the government. There was only one official political party—the Communist party, led by Josef Stalin. People expressing other views were often sent to jail or forced from their homes.

On February 9, 1946, Stalin addressed the people of his country. He blamed capitalism for World War II. He also said that there would never be peace as long as capitalists were in power anywhere in the world. Americans were scared.

As World War II ended, the Soviets occupied much of Eastern Europe and Iran. They were making inroads in the Far East. Some people in the United States felt that the Soviet Union was trying to take over the world.

The Soviets had made an agreement that they would remove all troops from Iran by March 2, 1946. However, their troops remained until Truman sent what he called "a blunt message" to Stalin.[2] In the message Truman insisted that the Soviets withdraw their troops. On March 24 Stalin announced that the troops would be removed.

The right of the Soviet Union to stay in Eastern Europe was established at a conference with the Soviets, Great Britain, and the United States early in 1945. The Soviets promised free elections, but they did not keep their word. The United States could do little to enforce it without risking the start of a war.

At home supplies of food and consumer goods were still low while prices were high. Beef prices were so expensive that some people ate horse meat.[3] Because of these problems at home and overseas, Truman's popularity dropped sharply. His approval rating, once at 87 percent, had dropped to 32 percent by October 1946.[4]

Those who had believed that Truman could never fill Roosevelt's shoes seem to be right. Long ago, playwright William Shakespeare wrote a line that has become famous. It reads, "To err is human." The definition of the word err is to make a mistake. In 1946 Americans were saying "To err is Truman."

Truman was not up for reelection in November 1946, but many Democratic congressmen and senators were. With Truman unpopular, his Democratic party was clobbered in the elections. The Republicans became the majority party in both the House of Representatives and the Senate. It was the first time that Republicans controlled both the House and Senate since before World War II. Just days after the election, Truman ended nearly all wage and price controls.

Because of the labor unrest, the new Congress passed a strong anti-union law in 1947. It was sponsored by two conservative Republicans, Senator Robert Taft from Ohio and Representative Fred A. Hartley, Jr., from New Jersey. Called the Taft-Hartley Act, it decreased some of the unions' powers.

Previously some unions demanded that only union workers be hired on jobs. That practice is known as a "closed shop." The Taft-Hartley Act made this practice illegal. The act also stated that any strike that would cause a national emergency must be delayed for eighty days.

Truman supported the unions who opposed the Taft-Hartley Act. He vetoed the bill, but it was passed over his veto by the Republican Congress.

It was a very lonely time for Truman. That was not only for political reasons. Bess and Margaret did not like Washington, D.C. Unlike many First Ladies, Bess Truman had no interest in a public life. She and Margaret lived some of the time in Independence, leaving the President alone in Washington. It is no surprise that Truman referred to the White House as "the great white prison" and the "great white jail."[5]

In his diary he described the routine of his day. The men he refers to here, John and Barnett, were White House servants.

The President wrote:

> Had dinner by myself tonight. . . . Barnett in tails and white tie pulls out my chair, pushes me up to the table. John in tails and white tie brings me a fruit cup. Barnett takes away the empty cup. John brings me a plate, Barnett brings me a tenderloin, John brings me asparagus, Barnett brings me carrots and beets. I have to eat alone and in silence in candle lit room. I ring—Barnett takes away the plate and butter plates. John comes in with a napkin and silver crumb tray—there are no crumbs but John has to brush them off the table anyway. Barnett brings me a plate with a finger bowl and doily on it. . . . I take a hand bath in the finger bowl and go back to work. What a life![6]

Shortly after the 1946 elections, Truman came down with a cold. His doctor advised him to take a vacation. A naval base commandant's home in Key West, Florida, was suggested. Truman fell in love with the hot tropics and palm trees. The sprawling white building in Key West soon became his winter escape from the cold dampness of Washington.

Truman also took a bold step that winter, which surprised and angered many members of his own party. Since the end of the war he had heard reports about African-American veterans being beaten in southern states. He said, "My God. I had no idea it was as terrible as that. We've got to do something."[7]

The Little White House, in Key West, Florida became Harry Truman's winter escape from the cold dampness of Washington, D.C.

He created a President's Committee on Civil Rights on December 5, 1946. The members were assigned to investigate racial violence and the status of civil rights in America. Was this the same person who once wrote and said racist statements? The committee would spend much of the next year studying the matter.

In Europe the winter was proving to be very brutal. People there were still recovering from the carnage of World War II. Extreme cold weather caused energy shortages and possible food shortages for the spring. Two countries, Greece and Turkey, had been supported by Great Britain. Now the British had their own problems, and could no longer support other countries.

It was felt that something had to be done or the Soviet Union would fill the vacuum caused by the vacating British. That would mean Greece and Turkey would fall to communism.

On March 12 Truman announced that the United States would give moral and economic aid to Greece and Turkey. He added that they would do the same for any other democratic country in danger of falling under communist rule. This became known as the Truman Doctrine. It was approved by Congress.

Less than three months later the Truman Doctrine was expanded. Truman's Secretary of State George C. Marshall announced another plan. It was to offer financial aid to any country in Europe that needed to rebuild.

The Soviet Union rejected the aid, so it went only to democratic countries. Germany and Italy, who fought against the United States in World War II, accepted it. This policy became known as the Marshall Plan. It was also known as the European Recovery Program.

Truman's policy of helping other nations kept communism from spreading. Citizens happy with their way of life would have no reason to look for another form of government.

On the other hand, the United States would not invade an existing communist country to force change. Americans had had enough of war. The policy of controlling the further spread of communism was called "containment."

Meanwhile the President's Committee on Civil

Rights published its findings in October 1947. It found much discrimination against African Americans. The committee offered over thirty recommendations to fix the situation.

Southern citizens were outraged. A Baptist minister in Jacksonville, Florida, told Truman, "If that report is

President Harry S. Truman shakes hands with Secretary of State George C. Marshall at Washington, D.C. National Airport.

carried out, you won't be elected dogcatcher in 1948. The South today is the South of 1861."[8]

Such threats did not stop Truman. On February 2, 1948, he asked Congress to enact some of the recommendations. Most concerned making it easier for African Americans to vote in the South. Throughout the South there were laws making it difficult for African Americans to vote.

The issue of bigotry was also behind a serious issue overseas. During World War II about 6 million Jews were murdered by the Nazis. They were not battle casualties, but part of a racist plan by Hitler to rid the world of all Jews. This is now known as the Holocaust.

Once the war ended many surviving European Jews moved to Palestine, the Biblical Jewish homeland in the Middle East. At the time Palestine was under rule of Great Britain. The Jews hoped to make Palestine a modern Jewish homeland. Most Jews believed that only in their own nation, where they could govern themselves, would they be safe from another Holocaust.

A homeland for the Jews in Palestine was supported by the British in a document released in 1917 called the Balfour Declaration. However, no homeland was ever created. Now that they had suffered so much in the war, Jews were even more determined to have their own nation.

Yet 1.3 million Arabs were already living in Palestine.[9] Most Arabs believed that a Jewish nation would violate their rights. Jews and Arabs had numerous skirmishes over the land. The members of the United Nations voted for a compromise solution. Palestine would be divided into Arab and Jewish sections. The Jewish section would become the nation of Israel. The compromise would have to be approved by two thirds of the countries that belonged to the United Nations.

Some Americans believed that it was only fair that the Jews have their own nation as others do. Truman's old friend and business partner Eddie Jacobson was one. He visited Truman and urged the President to support the Jewish state.

Others said that Palestine was not big enough to support a Jewish home without hurting the Arabs already living there. Many felt both sides had good points.

On May 14, 1948, Great Britain officially gave up its control of Palestine. At 6:00 P.M. that day Israel declared its independence. At 6:11 P.M. the United States formally recognized Israel. It was the first nation to do so.

No sooner had one fire been put out then Truman had another on his hands. This time it was again in Europe.

The Marshall Plan was in operation. Trucks were delivering food and fuel to the parts of Berlin occupied by the Allies. There was a problem, however. To make the deliveries, the trucks had to drive through Soviet-controlled East Germany.

On June 24, 1948, the Soviet Union refused to allow

Allied trucks to cross its territory and enter Berlin. This type of action is called a blockade. With the blockade in effect, the people of Berlin could not get supplies.

The Soviets had no intention of letting up. Truman could have taken a harsh stance and risked a threat of war. Or he could have given in to the Soviets. By doing that, he would have turned Berlin over to the communists.

Instead, Truman and his advisers came up with a

SOURCE DOCUMENT

This Government has been informed that a Jewish state has been proclaimed in Palestine, and recognition has been requested by the provisional Government thereof.

The United States recognizes the provisional government as the de facto authority of the new State of Israel.

Harry Truman

Approved
May 14, 1948.

Harry Truman signed this draft of a press release on May 14, 1948, recognizing Israel. The United States was the first nation to do so.

clever idea. Cargo airplanes would be used to deliver supplies to the people of Berlin. This became known as the "Berlin Airlift."

The presidential election of 1948 was approaching. At first Truman was not sure whether he would run for another term. Two reasons explain why he decided to do so. One was that he believed in Franklin D. Roosevelt's New Deal programs. He was concerned that they could be wiped out by a Republican President and a Republican Congress. The other was that Truman wanted to be elected President on his own.[10] Many still saw him as an accidental President.

Shortly after being chosen as the Democratic nominee for President, Truman made two landmark civil rights decisions. On July 26 he ordered an end to segregation in the armed forces. Then he outlawed discrimination in the hiring of federal workers.

Though Thomas E. Dewey had a huge lead in the polls, Truman did have supporters. The fact that he vetoed the Taft-Hartley Act made labor unions favor him. One union leader who publicly supported Truman was the president of the Screen Actors Guild (SAG) Ronald Reagan. SAG is the union representing movie actors.

In a political advertisement Reagan said, "This is Ronald Reagan speaking to you from Hollywood. You know me as a motion picture actor. But tonight I am just a citizen pretty concerned about the national election next month and more than a little impatient with the

★ SECURE THE PEACE ★

ELECT
★ HARRY S. TRUMAN ★
PRESIDENT

This 1948 presidential campaign poster shows a confident looking Harry Truman.

promises the Republicans made before they got control of Congress a couple of years ago."[11]

Enough Americans voted for Truman. When he took the oath of office on January 20, 1949, he was President in his own right. In addition, the Democrats won back both houses of Congress.

One of the country's biggest newspapers, The *Chicago Tribune*, was confident on election night that Truman would lose. Although not all of the votes had been counted, the *Tribune* ran a large headline that read: "DEWEY DEFEATS TRUMAN." As Truman stood in the back of a train in the St. Louis railroad station the morning after the election, he was presented a copy of the *Tribune*. President Truman held the newspaper high and smiled.

7

A WARM WELCOME AND A COLD WAR

B y now the American people had gotten to know Harry Truman. Americans were no longer bothered by him not being Franklin Roosevelt. In fact, many liked Truman's plain manner of speaking.

He came across as a no-nonsense President. Truman was viewed as a man who pulled no punches and did what he said. His manner charmed the public, as it had charmed Tom Pendergast fifteen years earlier. However, he was known to pepper his language with cursing now and then. Some felt that this was not presidential.

After the hectic 1948 campaign, Truman took another trip to Key West for some needed rest. Key West was the place where he could unwind. There he would wear a loud flashy shirt instead of a jacket and tie. He spent his days fishing and sailing instead of sitting in an office. For dinner there was often a relaxing barbecue. Afterwards he might join friends in a game of cards on the south porch.

The Trumans had yet another new home as soon as they arrived back in Washington. For some time they had been hearing creaks and groans from the wooden floors in the White House. Then a leg from Margaret's piano crashed through the floor of her White House bedroom. After nearly one hundred and fifty years of use, the grand building was in need of repair.

Almost the entire interior had to be gutted and refurbished. The Trumans were forced to move. They

A leg from Margaret Truman's piano crashed through her White House bedroom floor in 1948. This led to the complete remodeling of the Executive Mansion. Here the piano is shown at the Harry S. Truman National Historic Site.

took up residence across the street in a much smaller building called Blair House. It was used mainly to house important visitors. The small size of Blair House might have caused trouble for a large family. However, Bess stayed mostly in Independence. Margaret had started a singing career, and was often out on tour. So the size of Blair House was not a problem.

Every January the President goes before Congress to deliver a speech called the State of the Union message. In it the President discusses the condition of the country. He also outlines policies for the coming year. Truman gave his 1949 State of the Union address on January 5.

In his message Truman called for a continuation of social programs to be paid for by the government. Included were low-income housing, raising the minimum wage, support for education, and a national health insurance program.

National health insurance meant that every citizen of the United States would have access to health care regardless of income. People would not be kept from getting medical care because they could not afford it. Doctors' and other health care workers' bills would be paid for by a government fund. The money in the fund would come from taxes.

These proposals were in line with the New Deal policies of Franklin D. Roosevelt. Truman had made similar ones before. Because Truman was viewed by many as an accidental President, his ideas were not taken seriously.

The Truman family was forced to move to Blair House, shown here, while the White House was being remodeled.

Now that he was President in his own right, his views were given more respect. Truman even gave his group of programs a name. He called them "the Fair Deal."

In the wake of his surprise election, Truman's approval rating jumped to 69 percent. It was his highest rating in three years.[1] Things looked promising for the new term.

Truman and most Americans were still concerned about the possible spread of communism into Western Europe. So Truman asked the State Department to draft a treaty with other democracies. Secretary of State Dean Acheson got busy drawing up the treaty, with help from

British Foreign Secretary Ernest Bevin. The treaty stated that any nation signing it would defend any other such nation if attacked by a communist country. These nations became the North Atlantic Treaty Organization (NATO).

The other original members of NATO were: Belgium, Canada, Denmark, France, Iceland, Italy, Luxembourg, the Netherlands (Holland), Norway, Portugal, and the United Kingdom (England, Scotland, Wales, and Northern Ireland). In later years Greece, Turkey, West Germany, and Spain joined.

Though others did most of the writing of the treaty, it was up to Truman to convince both the American people and Congress to approve it. The treaty sailed through both houses of Congress. Truman later claimed that NATO and the Marshall Plan were his proudest achievements as President.[2]

In mid-May Truman received a belated birthday present. It was news that the Soviet blockade of Berlin was over. The Berlin Airlift was a smashing success. Over two hundred and seventy thousand flights of mercy were made. Over 2 million tons of food and other necessary supplies were delivered.[3] Patience had won out. War was avoided.

At home several of Truman's modest Fair Deal proposals were approved by the new Congress. The minimum wage was raised, and a Housing Act was passed. Through this act about 810,000 low-income homes were built.[4]

Yet Truman's most daring ideas were stopped. One was national health insurance. Truman put a staff member named Oscar Ewing in charge of the health insurance program. Union workers and liberal Democrats favored it. Conservative Republicans and doctors were strongly against it.

Many doctors fearful of losing ultra-high incomes used the fear of communism to scare people into resisting Truman's plan. In part because of this opposition, the national health insurance idea failed.

By 1950 the fear of communism was running rampant in the United States. A Republican senator from Wisconsin named Joseph McCarthy was ready to exploit that fear. On February 9 he gave a speech in West Virginia. In it he held up a piece of paper, and said that it contained 205 names of Communist party members who worked for the United States State Department.[5]

In the days afterwards McCarthy made similar claims. There was no truth to any of them. Yet by making them, McCarthy brought a great deal of attention to himself.

With the Truman Doctrine, the Marshall Plan, and NATO in place, communism was being contained in Europe. However, trouble was brewing in another part of the world.

Just as Europe had been ravaged by Germany during World War II, China was devastated by Japan. After the war there was civil war in China, with communists trying to take over the country. By 1949 the communists had won.

On a peninsula bordering China is the country of Korea. Following World War II the United States and the Soviet Union were unable to agree on a single government to control Korea.

Korea was divided in two parts. North Korea would be communist and allied with the Soviet Union. South Korea was democratic and allied with the United States. The borderline separating North and South Korea was the 38th Parallel.

President Truman was relaxing at his home in Missouri during a short vacation in June 1950. On Saturday evening, June 24, the phone rang. Dean Acheson, the secretary of state, was on the line.

Acheson said, "Mr. President. I have very serious news. The North Koreans have invaded South Korea."[6]

Daughter Margaret later wrote, "None of us got much sleep that night. My father made it clear, from the moment he heard the news, that he feared this was the opening round in World War III."[7]

The United Nations immediately held meetings. On June 27 the UN recommended that its members provide military aid to South Korea. A total of sixteen nations contributed to the military effort. The United States provided most of the fighting forces. The Korean War had begun.

The attack by the North Korean communists spurred on Senator McCarthy. He claimed that the invasion happened because the Truman administration was filled with communists. Many Americans believed him.

Officially, the fighting in Korea was never called a war. Only Congress can declare war, and Truman never asked Congress to do so. Instead it was labeled a "police action."

In charge of the military effort was General Douglas MacArthur, a hero of World War II. MacArthur was a handsome dashing man and a skilled general. He fit perfectly the image of the spit-and-polish soldier.

By late September the UN forces under MacArthur had pushed the North Koreans back to the 38th Parallel. The original goal had been met. The Korean War could have been over.

But Truman, MacArthur, and the American people were filled with the spirit of victory.[8] Truman, most of his staff, and MacArthur decided not to stop. On September 27 a decision was made to enter North Korea. The new plan was to force the communists out of North Korea and unify the country. This was far different from the original goal.

The UN forces seemed to be on their way towards reaching their aim. Then, on the morning of November 1, Truman received an unconfirmed report that communist China had sent soldiers into North Korea to fight against UN troops.[9]

If the report was true, American soldiers were going to be in much more danger. Yet Truman could not have known that his own life was in danger that day.

At dawn on the morning of October 15, 1950, Harry Truman is met at Wake Island by General Douglas MacArthur.

Unlike the White House, Blair House sits close to the street. At 2:19 P.M. outside Blair House a gunfight broke out. Two men were trying to shoot their way into Blair House. Their plan was to kill the President.

Within three minutes it was over. A total of twenty-seven shots had been fired.[10] A White House police officer named Leslie Coffelt was shot and died later that day. Two other White House police officers were shot but survived.

One of the would-be assassins, Griselio Torresola, was killed. The other, Oscar Collazo, was shot but survived. Torresola and Collazo were born in Puerto Rico, an island in the Caribbean Sea. They had moved to New York City.

They belonged to an extremist group that wanted independence for Puerto Rico. (Puerto Rico is a commonwealth of the United States, which means that it has its own government, but is associated with the United States.)

The President was never in any danger. The surviving would-be assassin, Oscar Collazo, was sentenced to death for the killing of Coffelt. Truman later commuted the sentence to life imprisonment.

Aside from that brush with death, Truman had much on his mind late in 1950. His Fair Deal proposals were taking a back seat to the Korean War effort. By late November it was definitely known that communist China had entered the war. China had a powerful fighting force. The "easy war" in Korea was not going to be so easy after all.

Then, on the evening of December 5, Truman's boyhood friend and press secretary Charlie Ross died suddenly of a heart attack. While informing reporters of his friend's death, Truman choked up. In the middle of the first sentence, he began crying.[11] He was unable to finish what he wanted to say. Truman apologized to the reporters and went back to his office.

That evening Margaret gave a concert in Constitution Hall, a famous auditorium in Washington, D.C. The music critic for the *Washington Post*, Paul Hume, published his review of her concert in the next day's paper.

Hume wrote that Margaret was a horrible singer. He stated, "Miss Truman cannot sing very well. She is flat a good deal of the time. . . . There are few moments during her recital when one can relax and feel confident that she will make her goal, which is the end of the song."[12]

The President fumed when he read the review. He dashed off a vicious letter to Hume. Truman wrote, "Some day I hope to meet you. When that happens you'll need a new nose, a lot of beefsteak for black eyes, and perhaps a supporter below."[13]

Perhaps the stress of the news from Korea and the death of Charlie Ross had taken its toll on Truman. Most Americans did not care. They were outraged by the

SOURCE DOCUMENT

THE WASHINGTON POST
Wednesday, December 6, 1950

Postlude

Margaret Truman Sings Here Again With Light Program

By Paul Hume

Margaret Truman, soprano, sang in Constitution Hall last night.

It was not her first recital there, and it was probably not her last. Miss Truman is a unique American phenomenon with a pleasant voice of little size and fair quality.

She is extremely attractive on the stage. Her program is usually light in nature, designed to attract those who like the singing of Jeanette MacDonald and Nelson Eddy. Yet Miss Truman cannot sing very well.

She is flat a good deal of the time—more last night than at any time we have heard her in past years. There are few moments during her recital when one can relax and feel confident that she will make her goal, which is the end of the song.

Miss Truman has not improved in the years we have heard her. She has learned about her diaphragm and its importance to her singing. She has learned that she must work in order to make something of her voice. But she still cannot sing with anything approaching professional finish.

She communicates almost nothing of the music she presents. Schumann, Schubert, and Mozart were on her program last night. Yet the performance of music by these composers was no more than a caricature of what it would be if sung by any one of a dozen artists today.

And still the public goes and pays the same price it would for the world's finest singers.

It was wise and very sensible of this young American to open her program with three songs by Francis Hopkinson. For Hopkinson not only is numbered among the signers of the Declaration of Independence, but he is also counted as our first native composer.

A Waltz Song by Edward German was not worth resurrecting,

not Gverd Besley and Spross songs in the final group.

It is an extremely unpleasant duty to record such unhappy facts about so honestly appealing a person. But as long as Miss Truman sings as she has for three years, and does today, we seem to have no recourse unless it is to omit comment on her programs altogether.

Herman Allison gave fine accompaniments, but played two solos and an encore quite badly. Miss Truman's first encores were by Popper and Delibes, from whom she sang songs arranged from instrumental works. Her final encores were Grieg's My Johann, and Sweethearts, by Romberg.

President, Mrs. Truman, Atlee Hear Margaret

By the United Press

President and Mrs. Truman and British Prime Minister Clement Attlee were among an enthusiastic audience which packed Constitution Hall last night to hear Margaret Truman's concert. Attlee sat in the Presidential box as a guest of the President. With them also were the British Ambassador, Sir Oliver Franks, and Lady Franks.

Paul Hume's review of Margaret Truman's performance at Constitution Hall appeared in the Washington Post.

letter, and felt that the President should not conduct himself in that manner.

The President was not finished with controversy. The Korean War continued with neither side making any real gains. In early spring of 1951 General MacArthur seemed to be taking war matters into his own hands. However, the President of the United States is also the Commander in Chief of the Armed Forces. It was up to Truman, not MacArthur, to set policy. It was up to MacArthur to answer to Truman.

In March, Truman drew up a cease-fire proposal. He was going to submit it to the other nations fighting with the United States. A few days later MacArthur announced that he might expand the war beyond Korea into China. This was directly opposite to what the President was planning.

Truman later wrote about MacArthur's statement, "It was in open defiance of my orders as President and as Commander in Chief. . . . By this act MacArthur left me no choice—I could no longer tolerate his insubordination."[14]

Truman fired MacArthur from his job. A general named Matthew B. Ridgway was chosen to take MacArthur's place.

Reaction from the public was strongly against Truman. MacArthur was a well-loved war hero. Numerous Americans saw MacArthur as defending freedom against communism. Some believed that Truman's actions were traitorous. A poll taken soon after the firing showed that Americans thought MacArthur was unfairly fired. The margin was 69 to 29 percent.[15]

Senator Joseph McCarthy milked the situation for all he could. He now attacked former secretary of state and current Secretary of Defense George Marshall. Marshall was a World War II hero for whom Truman had the greatest respect.

SOURCE DOCUMENT

77 Statement and Order by the President on Relieving General MacArthur of His Commands. *April 11, 1951*

[1.] *Statement by the President:*

With deep regret I have concluded that General of the Army Douglas MacArthur is unable to give his wholehearted support to the policies of the United States Government and of the United Nations in matters pertaining to his official duties. In view of the specific responsibilities imposed upon me by the Constitution of the United States and the added responsibility which has been entrusted to me by the United Nations, I have decided that I must make a change of command in the Far East. I have, therefore, relieved General MacArthur of his commands and have designated Lt. Gen. Matthew B. Ridgway as his successor.

Full and vigorous debate on matters of national policy is a vital element in the constitutional system of our free democracy. It is fundamental, however, that military commanders must be governed by the policies and directives issued to them in the manner provided by our laws and Constitution. In time of crisis, this consideration is particularly compelling.

General MacArthur's place in history as one of our greatest commanders is fully established. The Nation owes him a debt of gratitude for the distinguished and exceptional service which he has rendered his country in posts of great responsibility. For that reason I repeat my regret at the necessity for the action I feel compelled to take in his case.

This April 11, 1951 statement from President Truman relieved General MacArthur of his command in Korea.

Truman ignored McCarthy's charges, hoping that they would end soon. Although angered by them, he refused to comment one way or another to the press.[16] At one point Secretary of Agriculture Clinton Anderson privately told Truman that he had a file on McCarthy. Anderson said that it contained embarrassing facts about McCarthy, including evidence of extramarital affairs. Anderson suggested leaking the file to the press in hopes that it would ruin McCarthy.

Truman did not approve of such dirty tricks. A writer named John Hersey wrote that Truman said, "Nobody, not even the president of the United States, can approach too close to a skunk, in skunk territory, and expect to get anything out of it except a bad smell."[17]

As Truman's second term was coming to a close in 1952, steel workers threatened to strike. Truman felt a steel strike would be disastrous for a nation at war. He used his power to seize the mills. That means that the government took over the mills, planning to operate them.

Nearly two months later the Supreme Court ruled that Truman had misused his power. Immediately after the decision, steel workers did go on strike. It lasted seven weeks and was the longest and costliest steel strike in the country's history.[18]

8

TRUMAN'S TWILIGHT YEARS

Truman could have run for another term as President. But he was not popular in 1952. The Korean War was dragging on, and Americans were frustrated. The United States had proven its military might in World War II. Yet it appeared that it was unable to win a war in a little country like Korea.

The steel strike left a bitter taste in people's mouths. Fear of communism was widespread. On top of that there were corrupt actions taking place within Truman's administration.

The corruption cases mainly involved people in high positions using power to receive gifts or favors. One case involved Truman's military aide, a general named Harry Vaughan. Vaughan gave special favors to businesspeople. In exchange he sometimes received gifts.

To the President, these incidents were minor violations. He called them "flyspecks."[1] Republicans, however, seized upon these cases. They referred to the corruption as "the mess in Washington." Some hinted that the root of the corruption was Truman himself. By early 1952 Truman's approval rating was at an all-time low. It stood at 23 percent.[2]

Truman decided not to run for another term. To replace him, the Democrats chose Adlai Stevenson, the governor of Illinois. Stevenson's opponent was General Dwight D. Eisenhower, perhaps the country's most admired hero of World War II. Both Stevenson and Eisenhower took moderate positions for their parties.

Even though Truman was not running, Eisenhower and the Republicans made the Truman administration the target of their campaign. They spoke out about the ongoing Korean War, the spread of communism, and the corruption of the Truman staff. Eisenhower won an easy victory.

By the time Eisenhower took office, Truman was no longer one of the general's admirers. He had had a falling out with Eisenhower. There were several reasons, but the biggest stemmed from Senator Joseph McCarthy's attack on General George Marshall.

In 1952 Eisenhower was planning to give a campaign speech with a few lines defending Marshall. However, his aides told him to cut those lines so that he would not offend McCarthy. Eisenhower did so, and Truman was furious.

Truman later wrote:

> General George C. Marshall . . . who was not only one of the most decent and honorable men this country has ever produced, and the creator of the wonderful Marshall Plan that helped save Europe and put it back on its feet, but also the man who had done more for Eisenhower than anyone else on earth.[3]

Dwight D. Eisenhower was inaugurated as the thirty-fourth President on January 20, 1953. On that day the Trumans left for home in Independence. The Trumans were not going to live in a mansion with servants. They were going to live as they had before Harry Truman was President.

After leaving the presidency, Harry Truman retired to his Independence, Missouri home. The living room of the house is shown here. The portrait above the fireplace by Jay Wesley Jacobs was the first portrait of President Harry Truman.

The morning after Truman returned home, he took a walk in his neighborhood. A reporter asked him what was the first thing he did after coming home. Truman answered simply, "I carried the grips up to the attic."[4] (A grip is another word for suitcase.)

Truman tried to return to a normal life. It was not easy. Businesses offered him huge salaries to head or represent their companies. He turned them down. Truman liked simple things. He enjoyed walking each morning at around 5:30. After his walk he would return home to catch up on mail. Then he would have breakfast.

Truman would then travel to an office he kept in a federal building in Kansas City. He used it as a place to meet visitors and write correspondence. However, there were problems when he tried to eat lunch in a public restaurant. People wanted to talk to Truman or get his autograph. It was inconvenient for both the President and the restaurant. So it was arranged that Truman would eat his meals at a private club in Kansas City.

In Washington, Joseph McCarthy continued his attacks. By this time, the public and the Senate had had enough. In December 1954, McCarthy was censured by the Senate for conduct unbecoming a senator. McCarthy died in 1957. The practice of accusing people without showing evidence is today known as "McCarthyism."

Truman's first major project out of the White House was writing his memoirs of his years as President. It was an immense job. Truman separated his memoirs into two volumes. The first came out in the fall of 1955. It covered Truman's first year in office and was subtitled *Year of Decisions.* The second volume was released in the spring of 1956. It dealt with the rest of his presidency and was subtitled *Years of Trial and Hope.*

This was a happy time for the ex-President. On April 21, 1956, daughter Margaret was married. Her husband was Clifton Daniel, a news editor with the *New York Times.* While his daughter and son-in-law were on their honeymoon, Harry and Bess took off on a seven-week trip to Europe. They considered this trip to be their own real honeymoon.

Truman continued to enjoy retirement. On June 5, 1957, he became a grandfather when a son was born to Margaret. A month later the Truman family could boast of something else new. The Harry S. Truman Presidential Library was opened just a mile from the Truman home in Independence. It was just the second modern presidential library. (Franklin Roosevelt's was the first, but Roosevelt died before it was opened.)

The former President now maintained an office in his library. There were no more problems of finding privacy at lunch. With home just a mile away, he ate lunch in his own kitchen with Bess.

He was in demand more and more as a speaker and guest. A friend said of Truman, "He's so damn happy that it makes me happy just being around him."[5]

In May 1960 he became a grandfather again when Margaret had another boy. And in November, 1960, a

Democrat was once again elected President. It was John F. Kennedy, senator from Massachusetts.

The tension over Berlin that began in 1948 reached a head in 1961. Large numbers of East Berlin residents were escaping their homes to live in freedom in West Berlin. So many were leaving that the communists raised a huge concrete wall to separate East and West Berlin. Escape now was nearly impossible. This became known as the "Berlin Wall."

President Kennedy was assassinated in 1963. At the funeral, Truman and Eisenhower sat in the same pew. Reporters wrote that the two former Presidents were friends again. However, Margaret Truman said that

The signing of the Medicare Bill at the Truman Library was attended by President Johnson, Vice-President Humphrey, former President Truman, Mrs. Johnson, Mrs. Truman, and others.

there never was a real feud between Truman and Eisenhower.[6]

Vice President Lyndon Johnson was now President. Johnson ran for President in his own right in 1964 and beat Republican Barry Goldwater in a landslide. On July 30, 1965, Johnson went to the Truman Library in Independence for a special ceremony. With Truman looking on, Johnson signed the Medicare bill into law. Medicare is a system of national health insurance for the elderly. It is a remnant of the national health insurance program that Truman tried, but failed, to pass.

Margaret Truman had two more sons in the 1960s, and Harry Truman was a proud grandfather. He continued to make regular trips to his presidential library office until 1967. By 1972 his body was failing him. Truman died on December 26, 1972, at age eighty-eight. Harry S. Truman was buried in the courtyard of his presidential library.

9

LEGACY: ONE OF THE GREATEST

When President Truman died in 1972, his reputation was on the upswing. Yet not even his greatest admirer would have believed the turnabout. Decades after leaving office Harry S. Truman is today respected as one of the ten greatest Presidents in United States history.

A survey of nearly eight hundred and fifty historians in 1982 ranked Truman as the nation's eighth best President.[1] The *Chicago Tribune* conducted a survey of forty-nine of the nation's "leading historians and political scholars" the same year.[2] Here also, Truman ranked eighth best.[3]

In January 1995, *USA Today Magazine* ran an article titled "Harry S. Truman: America's Last Great Leader?"[4]

In the 1980s and 1990s presidential candidates of

both major parties claimed Truman as a model. Republican Presidents Ronald Reagan and George Bush declared that the current Democrats had strayed from Truman's principles. (This was the same Ronald Reagan who blasted Republicans in that radio ad for Truman in 1948. He became a conservative and switched parties in the 1960s.)

Democrats such as Walter Mondale, Michael Dukakis, and Bill Clinton disagreed. They said that Truman would still be as anti-Republican as he was in his day.

Why have so many people embraced Truman? This is the President whom only 23 percent of the country thought was doing a good job when he was in office in 1952.[5]

For starters, the records of those who followed Truman in office include the Vietnam War, Watergate, the Iranian hostage crisis, and the Iran-Contra scandal. The corruption and failures during Truman's years in office seem minor compared to these failures and transgressions.

In addition history has shown most of Truman's important decisions to be correct ones. These include some that were unpopular at the time. Thanks to the Truman Doctrine, Greece and Turkey rejected communism. Thanks to the Marshall Plan, Western Europe was rebuilt and became a thriving region.

Even without NATO, Western Europe might have stayed free from communist attack. NATO insured it.

The Berlin Airlift, which fed the starving people of Berlin for nearly a year, is regarded as a skillful plan. (The Berlin Wall was torn down by Berlin residents in 1989. It was part of a rebellion that spelled the end of communism in the Soviet Union and Eastern Europe.)

Overall Truman's policy of containment was successful. No additional European countries became communist under Truman's watch. No major war was started in Europe.

There was one war, the undeclared one in Korea. Here Truman gets mixed marks. If one looks at the fact that the communists were driven out of South Korea, the war was a victory. If one looks at the fact that the war dragged on for two and a half years, the war was a partial failure. Most historians consider the Korean War a draw.

South Korea has since grown into a strong country. North Korea remains communist. Communist China has adopted a trial form of capitalism.

Most historians today think that Truman was correct to fire General MacArthur. It preserved the integrity of the office of the President. Some say it avoided a war with China that could have developed into World War III.

Truman's compassion for people is also given credit. The country of Israel has grown and prospered. Jews living with sanctioned bigotry in the Soviet Union and other countries have found welcoming homes in Israel.

However, General Marshall's warnings about Arab

resistance were correct. The Middle East has been a troubled region. There have been four wars and countless terrorist attacks involving the Arab countries and Israel.

Truman's civil rights policies have been praised. His decision to end racial discrimination in the armed services has been called the beginning of the modern civil rights movement. While some might question that claim, most would agree that the decision planted the seed of the movement.

President Bill Clinton tried to pass a national health care plan just as Truman did. It met the same result as Truman's proposal. Special interest groups ran a huge campaign opposing it. Among the most active were the insurance industry and political conservatives.

The most controversial legacy of the Truman years was the decision to drop atomic bombs on Japan to end World War II. It was the cause for much soul searching by Americans during the fiftieth anniversary of the decision in 1995.

All agreed that the atomic bomb was a horrible weapon. They admitted that those who died from the bomb attacks died awful deaths. But there was much discussion on whether it was necessary to use the bombs in order to win the war.

Some historians say that Japan would have surrendered without the bomb attacks. They said that the United States' reason for using the atomic bombs was vengeance. Some added that the United States bombed Japan because its residents are nonwhites.

Most historians disagree. They argue that Japan was not about to surrender. If the United States did not use the bomb, a land invasion would have been necessary to end the war. The result would have been a massive loss in American lives.

Truman gave a lecture twenty years after the war ended. In it he commented about his decision to use the atomic bombs. He said:

> It was a question of saving hundreds of thousands of American lives. I don't mind telling you that you don't feel normal when you have to plan hundreds and thousands of . . . deaths of American boys who are alive and joking and having fun. You break your heart and your head trying to figure out a way to save one life.[6]

He was later asked if he had misgivings about using the atomic bomb. Truman answered, "Hell yes! I've had a lot of misgivings. . . ."[7]

In 1960 Truman wrote, "I abhor war and I am opposed to any kind of killing—whether by atomic bomb or bow and arrow. War is killing on a mass scale and it is war that we must eliminate—or it will eliminate us."[8]

Truman's wife Bess outlived the President by nearly ten years. She died quietly at age ninety-seven in 1982. Margaret Truman became a successful author. Her published books include biographies of her parents and mystery novels based in Washington, D.C.

Harry Truman was devoted to his family and basic

values. That might be one more reason why he is so respected today.

In an interview in 1959 he said, "Three things corrupt a man: Power, money and women. I never had but one woman in my life, and she's right at home. I never wanted power, and I never had any money, so I don't miss it."[9] To many, that is just how a President should be.

Perhaps Truman's greatest legacy was proving that a common person could succeed as President. He did so by being himself. Once he was put in a position of power, Truman used his instincts to do what he thought was right. People today feel that most of the time his actions were right.

Chronology

1884—Born in Lamar, Missouri, on May 8.

1887—Family moved to farm in Grandview, Missouri.

1890—Family moved to Independence, Missouri.

1901—Graduated from high school.

1902—Moved to Kansas City.

1902—Worked various jobs before settling in banking.
-1906

1906—Moved back to family farm in Grandview, Missouri.

1917—Served in Army during World War I.
-1918

1919—Married Elizabeth (Bess) Wallace on June 28; opened haberdashery with Eddie Jacobson.

1922—Business went bankrupt; elected county judge for Jackson County, Missouri.

1924—Daughter Margaret born on February 17; lost reelection to judgeship.

1926—Elected as presiding county judge for Jackson County.

1934—Elected to United States Senate from Missouri.

1940—Reelected to United States Senate.

1941—Headed Truman Committee.

1944—Elected Vice President of the United States under Franklin D. Roosevelt.

1945—Became President of the United States when Roosevelt died on April 12; attended Potsdam Conference; World War II ended after atomic bombs were dropped on Hiroshima and Nagasaki, Japan.

1946—Nation crippled by numerous strikes, including those by steel, coal-mining, and railroad workers; Republicans won control of both houses of Congress in November elections; took first Key West working vacation.

1947—Truman Doctrine and Marshall plans enacted.

1948—Recognition of new nation of Israel; Berlin Airlift began; ended segregation in United States armed forces; reelected President in surprise victory.

1949—Moved to Blair House while White House was renovated; introduced Fair Deal; NATO formed; Berlin Airlift ended.

1950—Korean War began; unhurt in assassination attempt.

1951—Fired General Douglas MacArthur.

1952—Seized steel mills during strike.

1953—Left presidency on January 20.

1955—Published first volume of memoirs.

1956—Published second volume of memoirs.

1957—Harry S. Truman Presidential Library opened.

1965—Attended signing as Medicare became law.

1972—Died on December 26.

Chapter Notes

Chapter 1

1. David McCullough, *Truman* (New York: Simon & Schuster, 1992), p. 695.

2. *Class of the Twentieth Century*, television program, volume 4 (1945-1952), CEL Communications, Inc., and Arts and Entertainment Network, 1991.

3. Merle Miller, *Plain Speaking: An Oral Biography of Harry S. Truman* (New York: Berkley Books, 1984, original copyright, 1974), p. 279.

4. Harry S. Truman, *Mr. Citizen* (New York: Bernard Geis Associates, 1960), p. 149.

Chapter 2

1. Merle Miller, *Plain Speaking: An Oral Biography of Harry S. Truman* (New York: Berkley Books, 1984, original copyright, 1974), p. 46.

2. Robert H. Ferrell, ed., *The Autobiography of Harry S. Truman* (Boulder, Colo.: Colorado Associated University Press, 1980), p. 6.

3. Ibid.

4. Ibid., p. 8.

5. Ibid.

6. David McCullough, *Truman* (New York: Simon & Schuster, 1992), p. 41.

7. Miller, p. 30.

8. Ibid., pp. 32, 50.

9. Ibid., p. 45.

10. Robert H. Ferrell, *Truman: A Centenary Remembrance* (New York: The Viking Press, 1984), p. 34.

11. Miller, p. 53.

12. Ibid., p. 57.

Chapter 3

1. David McCullough, *Truman* (New York: Simon & Schuster, 1992), p. 66.

2. Ibid., p. 70.

3. Robert H. Ferrell, *Truman: A Centenary Remembrance* (New York: The Viking Press, 1984), p. 43.

4. Ibid., p. 46.

5. Margaret Truman, *Harry S. Truman* (New York: William Morrow & Co., 1973), p. 55.

6. Robert H. Ferrell, ed., *Dear Bess: The Letters From Harry to Bess Truman 1910-1959* (New York: W. W. Norton & Company, 1983), p. 39.

7. Personal interview with Michael Mann, Harry S. Truman National Historic Site, January 8, 1996.

8. Ferrell, *Dear Bess: The Letters From Harry to Bess Truman 1910-1959*, p. 40.

9. Ibid., pp. 40-41.

10. Personal interview with Michael Mann, Harry S. Truman National Historic Site, January 8, 1996; April 23, 1996.

11. Ibid.

12. Truman, p. 59.

13. Merle Miller, *Plain Speaking: An Oral Biography of Harry S. Truman* (New York: Berkley Books, 1984, original copyright, 1974), p. 97.

14. Ibid.

Chapter 4

1. *Biography, Harry Truman*, television program, HTV Production and Arts and Entertainment Network, 1994.

2. Merle Miller, *Plain Speaking: An Oral Biography of Harry S. Truman* (New York: Berkley Books, 1984, original copyright, 1974), p. 126.

3. Robert H. Ferrell, ed., *Dear Bess: The Letters From Harry to Bess Truman 1910-1959* (New York: W. W. Norton & Company, 1983), p. 39.

4. Ibid.

5. Ibid., p. 254.

6. Miller, p. 130.

7. Alfred Steinberg, *The Man From Missouri: The Life and Times of Harry S. Truman* (New York: G. P. Putnam's Sons, 1962), p. 64.

8. Miller, p. 131.

9. *Biography, Harry Truman*, television program.

10. Robert H. Ferrell, *Truman: A Centenary Remembrance* (New York: The Viking Press, 1984), p. 76.

11. Russell D. Buhite and David W. Levy, *FDR's Fireside Chats* (New York: Penguin Books, 1993), p. 5.

12. Steinberg, p. 164.

13. Margaret Truman, *Harry S. Truman* (New York: William Morrow & Company, Inc., 1973), p. 117.

14. Ibid.

15. Ibid., p. 119.

16. Ferrell, *Truman: A Centenary Remembrance*, p. 101.

17. David McCullough, *Truman* (New York: Simon & Schuster, 1992), p. 247.

18. Ibid.

Chapter 5

1. Personal correspondence from Franklin D. Roosevelt Library, dated May 23, 1995.

2. *New York Times*, April 14, 1945, p. 4., per conversation with Liz Safly, researcher, Harry S. Truman Library, June 27, 1996.

3. James N. Giglio and Greg G. Thielen, *Truman in Cartoon and Caricature* (Ames, Iowa: Iowa State University Press, 1984), p. 14.

4. Roberta Page, "He Overcame Illness to Excel," *Independence Examiner*, "A Personal History of Harry S. Truman" special section, January 19, 1984, p. 12.

5. Giglio and Thielen, p. 14.

6. Robert H. Ferrell, ed., *Off the Record: The Private Papers of Harry S. Truman* (New York: Harper and Row, 1980), p. 55.

7. Alfred Steinberg, *The Man From Missouri: The Life and Times of Harry S. Truman* (New York: G. P. Putnam's Sons, 1962), p. 259.

8. Ferrell, *Off the Record*, p. 55.

9. David McCullough, *Truman* (New York: Simon & Schuster, 1992), p. 457.

10. Ibid.

Chapter 6

1. Robert H. Ferrell, *Truman: A Centenary Remembrance* (New York: The Viking Press, 1984), p. 188.

2. Harry S. Truman, *Memoirs by Harry S. Truman 1946-1952: Years of Trial and Hope: Volume 2* (New York: Da Capo Press, 1986, originally published New York: Doubleday & Co., 1956), p. 95.

3. Clifton Daniel, ed., *Chronicle of the 20th Century* (Liberty, Mo.: JL International Publishing, 1992), p. 615.

4. David McCullough, *Truman* (New York: Simon & Schuster, 1992), p. 520.

5. Robert H. Ferrell, *Off the Record: The Private Papers of Harry S. Truman* (New York: Harper and Row, 1980), pp. 2, 145, 256.

6. Ibid., pp. 168-169.

7. William E. Leuchtenburg, "The Conversion of Harry Truman," *American Heritage*, November 1991, p. 58.

8. Ibid., p. 60.

9. Daniel, p. 642.

10. McCullough, p. 585.

11. Ricki Green, executive producer, *The Great Upset of 1948*, television documentary, Greater Washington Educational Telecommunications Association, Inc., 1988.

Chapter 7

1. David McCullough, *Truman* (New York: Simon & Schuster, 1992), p. 727.

2. Ibid., p. 735.

3. Ibid., p. 734.

4. James N. Giglio and Greg G. Thielen, *Truman in Cartoon and Caricature* (Ames, Iowa: Iowa State University Press, 1984), p. 65.

5. Alfred Steinberg, *The Man From Missouri: The Life and Times of Harry S. Truman* (New York: G. P. Putnam's Sons, 1962), p. 371.

6. Ibid., p. 361.

7. Margaret Truman, *Harry S. Truman* (New York: William Morrow & Co., 1973), p. 455.

8. Ibid.

9. McCullough, p. 808.

10. George Sullivan, *They Shot the President* (New York: Scholastic, Inc., 1993), p. 112.

11. Margaret Truman, p. 500.

12. Ralph Keyes, *The Wit & Wisdom of Harry Truman* (New York: HarperCollins, 1995), p. 113.

13. Ibid.

14. Ibid.

15. Harry S. Truman, *Memoirs of Harry S. Truman 1946-1952: Years of Trial and Hope: Volume 2* (New York: Da Capo Press, 1986, originally published by Doubleday & Co., 1956), p. 442.

16. McCullough, p. 861.

17. Keyes, p. 108.

18. McCullough, p. 901.

Chapter 8

1. Joseph Gies, *Harry S. Truman: A Pictorial Biography* (Garden City, N.Y.: Doubleday & Co., 1968), p. 152.

2. David McCullough, *Truman* (New York: Simon & Schuster, 1992), p. 873.

3. Margaret Truman, *Where the Buck Stops: The Personal and Private Writings of Harry S. Truman* (New York: Warner Books, 1989), p. 71.

4. Paul F. Boller, Jr., *Presidential Anecdotes* (New York: Oxford University Press, 1981), p. 284.

5. McCullough, p. 965.

6. Margaret Truman, *Harry S. Truman* (New York: William Morrow & Co., 1973), p. 575.

Chapter 9

1. Robert K. Murray and Tim H. Blessing, "The Presidential Performance Study: A Progress Report," *The Journal of American History*, December 1983, p. 540.

2. Ibid., p. 536.

3. Ibid., p. 540.

4. Susanne A. Roschwalb and Gordon L. Smith, "Harry S. Truman: America's Last Great Leader?," *USA Today Magazine*, January 1995, p. 86.

5. David McCullough, *Truman* (New York: Simon & Schuster, 1992), p. 873.

6. Ralph Keyes, *The Wit & Wisdom of Harry Truman* (New York: HarperCollins, 1995), p. 92.

7. Ibid., p. 93.

8. Harry S. Truman, *Mr. Citizen* (New York: Bernard Geis Associates, 1960), p. 267.

9. Truman interview with *Washington Star*, May 3, 1959, as quoted in Harry S. Truman Library news release, undated.

Places to Visit

Connecticut

Museum of American Political Life, West Hartford. (860) 768-4090. The history of every presidential campaign in the United States is told through buttons, banners, photos, and videotape. Other exhibits are on topics such as third parties and the art of campaigning. Open year-round.

Florida

Little White House, Key West. (305) 294-9911. This is Truman's vacation retreat. Many furnishings are original. These include his living room desk and the poker table on the south porch. Open year-round.

Missouri

Harry S. Truman National Historic Site, Independence and Grandview. (816) 254-9929. The national historic site includes both the Delaware Street home in Independence and the family farm in Grandview. Guided tours of both houses are offered. Open year-round.

Harry S. Truman Courtroom and Office, Independence. (816) 795-8200. This is a courtroom Truman used as a county judge. You can tour his office and watch a multimedia show on Truman's years in Independence. Open year-round.

Harry S. Truman Library and Museum, Independence. (816) 833-1400. A highlight is a reproduction of the Oval Office. Video terminals, photos, touchscreens, and Truman's own possessions interpret his presidency. Open year-round.

Harry S. Truman Birthplace State Historic Site, Lamar. (417) 682-2279. You can tour the home where the thirty-third President was born. Open year-round.

Washington, D.C.

The White House. (202) 456-7041. Several rooms are open to visitors on certain weekday mornings. You can get tickets when you arrive, or in advance through your senator or congressperson. Open year-round.

Internet Addresses

Harry S. Truman Presidential Library

E-mail   library@truman.nara.gov

Home Page   http://sunsite.unc.edu/lia/president/truman.html

Harry S. Truman National Historic Site, The National Park System

Home Page   http://www.nps.gov/hstr/

Further Reading

Black, Wallace B., and Jean F. Blashfield. *Hiroshima and the Atomic Bomb*. New York: Crestwood House, 1993.

Ferrell, Robert H. (editor). *Dear Bess: The Letters from Harry to Bess Truman 1910-1959*. New York: W. W. Norton & Co., 1983).

Judson, Karen. *The Presidency of the United States*. Springfield, N.J.: Enslow Publishers, 1996.

Keyes, Ralph. *The Wit & Wisdom of Harry Truman*. New York: HarperCollins, 1995.

Regan, Geoffrey. *Israel and the Arabs*. Minneapolis: Lerner Publications, Co., 1986.

Stein, R. Conrad. *World War II in the Pacific: "Remember Pearl Harbor."* Springfield, N.J.: Enslow Publishers, 1994.

Steins, Richard. *Our Elections*. Brookfield, Conn.: Millbrook Press, 1994.

Sullivan, George. *They Shot the President*. New York: Scholastic, Inc., 1993.

Truman, Harry S. *Mr. Citizen*. New York: Bernard Geis Associates, 1960.

Truman, Margaret. *Harry S. Truman*. New York: William Morrow & Co., 1973.

———. *Where the Buck Stops: The Personal and Private Writings of Harry S. Truman*. New York: Warner Books, 1989.

Westerfeld, Scott. *The Berlin Airlift*. Englewood Cliffs, N.J.: Silver Burdett Press, 1989.

Index

MAI   **YA**

10/9/97